Table of Contents

4

To the Rescue!

Saint Bernards used to be rescue dogs.

They sniffed to find people who were lost in the snow.

Saint Bernards have thick fur
that keeps them warm.
They have large feet
that help them walk in snow.

From Puppy to Adult

Saint Bernard puppies love
to play in the snow.
They sniff and dig.

Saint Bernard puppies look
tiny next to their big mother.
They grow quickly.
At four months, they are
larger than most adult dogs.

Adult Saint Bernards
are some of the
world's biggest dogs.
They are about as tall
as a kitchen table.

Saint Bernard Care

Saint Bernards have oil
on their fur.
The oil makes their fur
waterproof in snow
and rain.

Saint Bernards need
a bath only when
they are very dirty.
Owners don't want to wash
the oil from their fur.

Saint Bernards are big dogs
with big bones.
They need dog food
that makes
their bones strong.

Saint Bernards can find
and fetch almost anything
for their owners.
Saint Bernards
are gentle giants.

Glossary

fetch—to go after something and bring it back

gentle—tame and kind; gentle animals are not rough.

oil—a slippery liquid that does not mix with water

rescue—to save someone who is lost or in danger

waterproof—keeping water out

Read More

Clutton-Brock, Juliet. *Dog.* DK Eyewitness Books. New York: DK Publishing, 2004.

Hall, Lynn. *Barry: The Bravest Saint Bernard.* Step into Reading. New York: Random House, 2003.

Internet Sites

FactHound offers a safe, fun way to find Internet sites related to this book. All of the sites on FactHound have been researched by our staff.

Here's how:

1. Visit *www.facthound.com*

2. Type in this special code **0736853375** for age-appropriate sites. Or enter a search word related to this book for a more general search.

3. Click on the **Fetch It** button.

FactHound will fetch the best sites for you!

Index

Word Count: 163
Grade: 1
Early-Intervention Level: 16

Editorial Credits

Martha E. H. Rustad, editor; Juliette Peters, designer; Wanda Winch, photo researcher; Scott Thoms, photo editor

Photo Credits

Cheryl A. Ertelt, cover; Corbis/Royalty-Free, 4; Elite Portrait Design/Lisa Fallenstein-Holthaus, 18; Getty Images Inc./Stone/Charles Thatcher, 20; Kent Dannen, 1, 8, 14, 16; Landov LLC/EPA/Olivier Maire, 6; Norvia Behling/Connie Summers, 12; Peter Arnold Inc./Malcolm S. Kirk, 10